THE WRESTLE

THE WRESTLE

David Tensen

*poems of divine disappointment
and discovery*

ST MACRINA PRESS

Author website: www.davidtensen.com
Author email: david@davidtensen.com

St Macrina Press
Abbotsford, BC, Canada

Wing illustration: Copyright © 2020 Andy Bridge
                    instagram @andybridgeillustrator

Edited: Felicia Murrell
                    www.yzcounsel.com

Also available in eBook and Audiobook format.

The Wrestle / David Tensen. -- 1st ed.
ISBN 978-0-6489893-2-5

Dedicated to those who refuse

to be let go of.

The courageous few

who brave the intimacy

of wrestling

God

themselves

and all that is in between.

Table of Contents

Introduction	1
A Blessing For The Heart Journey	6
On The Way Down	9
Ancient Paths	11
My Mask	14
Now+here	16
Count Your Losses	19
From Your Knees	22
The Brutality Of Brokeness	24
Found Its Place	26
The Light Responded	29
On God	31
The Wrestle	34
Kind Of Way	36
That Fire	40
Heart And Mind	42
Oh God	44
The Descent	46
So Close	49
Paradox Of Definition	51
And You Wait	53
Trinity Is	56
Displace Darkness	57
Control	58
As A Child	60
This Temple	61
On Empathy	63
The Burden Bearer – Piece 1	66
The Burden Bearer – Piece 2	69
Invisible Injury	72
My Story	74

Tender Heart   77
Who Took Your Voice – Piece 1   78
Who Took Your Voice – Piece 2   80
Who Took Your Voice – Piece 3   82
A Poem For Glenn   84
Another Poem For Glenn - Your Hand In Mine   85
The Convocation   87
On Boundaries   91
The Rescuer   92
Water Stories   94
Spinning On Empty   96
Letters   99
Elders   100
Dear Strength   102
Dear Breakdown   104
Dear Instruction   108
Dear Tears   110
Dear Joy   112
Dear Church   114
On Life   117
Held   118
That Photo Of You On Your First Day At School   120
A Good Ontology   124
Until You Forgive   125
I Want To Be   126
Time   127
The Seen Parent   128
Compani   130
Still   131
Never Vowed   132
Perfect Dad   134
The Past   136
Soap Film Prayer   138
A Blessing For The Heart Journey   140

ENDORSEMENTS

"A poet for these times, David Tensen articulates deeply the spectrum of my own personal thoughts, emotions, losses and issues. These words whisper transcendent rumors hidden in the viscera of humanity, lyrics of longing to be gratefully shared."
Wm. Paul Young – Author of *The Shack*

"David Tensen is a unique individual and a deep thinker whose words, flowing from his own experience penetrate deeply, causing one to stop, listen and reflect and to have conversations with God and with others. His words both uncover pain and bring healing, and at the same time, enable us to move one step forward or further on our journey."
James Condon – Commissioner Emeritus, Salvation Army, Australia

"Both the Jewish and Christian traditions have forever prayed their deepest heart-cries as poetry and their prophets offered us words when we only had groans. This is how I experience David Tensen. He's given us a prophetic Psalter apropos for these swirling times--a warm fire and bright light."
Bradley Jersak – Author of *A More Christlike God*

INTRODUCTION

I have a friend who refuses to publish her books electronically. Everyone tells her she could sell more if she moves beyond only publishing a physical book, but she refuses. When asked why, she explains that e-books don't find people. They don't end up on library shelves. They're not found in garage sales or on the shelves of old book exchange stores. They can't be loaned out and they rarely outlive the owner. Physical books, she says, have a mystical way of finding people.

Poetry found me a few years ago. Ironically, it wasn't via a book, but via a podcast interview with poet and philosopher David Whyte. I vividly remember the long street by my house where tears ran down my face as I heard him recite his poetry and carefully explain the origin of the piece. I listened to that long interview three times. It struck something inside of me, which only a poem may be able to explain. A week later I started penning and gingerly sharing my own poems.

Poetry found me when I most needed it. It gave me a way to shape experience and feelings that are beyond words, with words. I most needed it on the road to recovery from a season of compassion fatigue and burnout that I didn't think I'd ever find a way out of. Life and my own shortcomings had caught up with me. Only nine months earlier I had cancelled all my work-trips and all my appointments with those who wanted my time and spiritual/emotional expertise. I was done. Cooked. Fried. Bedridden and only making it through days with caffeine and Netflix documentaries.

A few months into my emotional crash, at the right time, a book my wife brought home from the library found me. A chapter in it made way for me to see the carefully hidden co-dependent parts of my soul that had got me this far in life - but were not fit for the next half. Hidden deep within me, was a part of me that was so tired and worn out, it had made itself a prison cell and refused to leave for anything other than a sympathetic ear and lots of rest. It was done rescuing others and trying to save the world at its own expense. It had driven me to be the atonement for many. This, in turn, came at a great cost to my wife, our three children and my own wellbeing.

It was several profound spiritual encounters with a loving triune God and the support of my wife and close friends that got me back on my feet and moving.

Perhaps this book has found you. My sincere prayer is that it helps give words to things you know to be true but haven't been able to express.

For my Christian and spiritual friends who read this, I hope these poems grant you courage to have more honest conversations with God. I have come to realise the important role that lament and raw honesty plays when it comes to our own maturity and relationship with God. Nearly half of the Psalms in our common Christian bible are songs of lament. Poems recited in dark places where truth is illuminated, and vindication is found. Yet today, we seldom hear a song or sing of how God disappointed us and has disappeared at the time we needed the most help.

How sad, that in the midst of worshipping the God of the breakthrough, we haven't been able to balance this with discovering the co-suffering God of the breakdown – particularly in evangelical streams. Being skilled crafters and wearers of masks seems the only way most of us make our way through life, hidden, until our act is over and our true selves demand attention. How gloriously messy and necessary those seasons are.

Within these lines of poetry, you will discover several themes. Themes that echo honest conversations with God. Themes of rescue and recovery. Pieces about life and parenting, plus several letters to emotions and a few that I've written with others in mind.

At the time of publishing, I can't say I've been writing poetry for very many years, but I do feel like some of these pieces have been within me for decades. I'm humbled to know you're spending your own time with me in this way. If time and effort permits, I'd love to hear how anything contained in these pages have spoken to you and helped you. You can email me personally at david@davidtensen.com.

It seems fitting to extend my deepest thanks and gratitude to all those who made this book possible. First, my patient and permission-giving wife Natalie and my three children, Mia, Willem and Cadell. You've enriched my life so much. Thank you, Paul, for making this book possible and for seeing its worth and place in the world. Thanks to Melissa, Andy, Dan and those who came alongside me during critical moments.

Finally, thank you to all those who financially and prayerfully supported Natalie and I for many years as we ran our not-for-profit organisation supporting leaders and bringing healing to many. I wouldn't be writing this without you.

The book opens with a blessing.

A BLESSING FOR THE HEART JOURNEY

Today, fellow fallers,
recoverers, rescuers,
winners, losers,
famous and infamous,
I bless you.

The runners and the lame,
the bankrupt and billionaires,
the saints and sinners,
the lost and lonely,
I bless you.

I bless you with knowing
that the journey of a thousand steps
will be paved by
potholes,
sinkholes,
assholes,
and whatever
it takes to make
you whole.
Because you are human.

I bless you with knowing
that the invitation
to face the world
with an unveiled face
may be done at your pace,
or never at all.
Because it's an invitation.

But know this:
By love and choice
Trinity's unmasked face
shines upon you
and is gracious to you.
Trinity lifts up their faces towards you
and offers you peace.
Because you belong.

David Tensen

ON THE WAY DOWN

Believe it or not, I have a degree in organisational leadership. I find the world of management theory and organisational change fascinating. What emerging theories demonstrate today is that effective and sustainable organisational changes occur in workplaces that are largely conversational, considerate and humane. On the contrary, organisational change becomes destructive when it is coercive, systems-focused and inhumane. As a result, managers are being forced to address shortcomings in their own maturity in order to successfully address and transcend shortcomings in the places they lead and manage. Not surprisingly, research shows there are no shortcuts to transformation both personally and corporately. Without question, change first requires a kind of deconstruction in order to make way for reconstruction.

Most epic stories and literature carry a common theme. Professor Joseph Campbell was an expert on comparative literature and comparative religion. Campbell's work became popularized when it was revealed that Campbell was consulted by George Lucas for the writing of the Star Wars sagas. His insight into mythology and the human experience are quite profound, including his work on the hero's journey which once again demonstrates that if one wishes to discover their true self, it is never without a painful quest towards dark nights and dragon lairs.

However it is delivered, whether through biblical narrative, change management theory, or mythological patterns found in epic tales, the common thread of truth seems to be that the journey towards transformational wholeness requires a painful descent towards unknown darkness, lament and liminality. If we stay on this downward path, we will come face-to-face with the truth of who we are and, I believe, who God is. Those who've ventured into the wilderness discover that God can be found in the depths of despair. I've come to experience, that when I'm most lost and in the deepest darkness, unable to see myself or the God I imagined would rescue me, only then can God's very Being illuminate the truth of who I am, and who God is as I Am.

The following pieces consider the gloriously disappointing and often painful journey downward to discovery that we are invited to walk on. Not just once, but time and time again we are invited to be held. Held in the midst of a wrestle.

ANCIENT PATHS

I thought
I could march
through life
guided by nothing
but my own steps.

Careful to only tread
on virgin ground
avoiding former tracks
and braving
unchartered estate.

With the cheer of fans
and the jeer of critics
at my back
I walked on
determined to find new land
and return to accolades
and told-you-so's.

But strong wind blew
and heavy rain fell
revealing the soil's secrets.

Footprints.
Everywhere,
footprints.
Traces on traces
from past eras.

Some foot trails ending
without warning.
Several turning back
on themselves.
Others stalling
at crossroads.
But, all before me
All around me
Footprints.

My head sunk
and pride with it.
Fists pounding the earth.
In anguish, I yelled to the Heavens:
This can't be so!

With a firm, quiet tone
Heaven replied:
But this must be so.
For you are on holy ground.

Made sacred by the footsteps
of forerunners
forebearers
forefathers
for you
Heaven continued:
Do you not know
that the very inner fire
which drove you
from the warmth
of your own tribe
was not lit by you,
but by divine desire
and hallowed birthright?

Can you now see that the storms
were a gift to uncover the truth?

...You were never meant
to forge new paths
on your own.
You were called
to uncover
ancient paths
and be guided
into the way
by me
and a great cloud
of witnesses.

MY MASK

The problem is
my mask fell off
when I went through that rough patch.
But I managed to put it back on really quick,
albeit a little crooked.

Then
the colours started to run
when I went through those storms.
But I found a brush and fixed it,
albeit a little messy.

Then
there was a time I lost it
when I went through that dark period.
But I found it before the morning,
albeit a little beat up.

Then
cracks started appearing
when I went through that dry spell.
But I found some sticky tape to mend it,
albeit sort of obvious now.

And now, the problem is
this crooked, messy, beat up and cracked mask
is all I've ever known.
But to be honest,
saving face is bloody hard work.

And
I have this sneaking suspicion
that the world
is not looking for me
to have my act together
but has been waiting
for me
to know
my act
is over.

NOW+HERE

It could feel
Like you are nowhere

For 40 minutes
For 40 days
40 years, perhaps.

One thing is certain:
At first
You will believe
You're lost.

If you're lucky
Loneliness and despair
Will tap you on the shoulder
Reminding you
Of their faithful presence.

Part of you
Will tell you
'This is the worst place.'
Part of you
Will know
Beyond thought
That this is where
You need to be;
In the middle
Of now+here

Now+here has much to offer you;
You have much to discover.
It has so much to say
About the sharp shadow
That follows you
Everywhere.
About all you avoid
All you turn to
And how you keep missing
Your true self
Waiting for you
In the wilderness.

In the desert
Fear and trembling
Are normal.
Those tales you heard
Of the strong
Losing their battles here,
They're all true.
You're supposed to lose.
You must surrender to the sun
And the wind
And the endless horizon.

Only then
When you're at your end
And you've fallen to embrace
Your sandy shadow
And faithful desert companions;
Only then
Will the manna fall
And the waters part
And the promise open up to you.

Only then
Will you know
How kind
And generous
A friend
Nowhere really is.

COUNT YOUR LOSSES

You could start by counting your losses.
Knowing that what's gone,
is gone.
It's important to let that happen
before you move on.
Like exhaling before you inhale again.
Otherwise, your lungs may explode.

Long ago, they burned things
or buried them.
Allowing them to return to creation.
Long ago,
we weren't so possessive.
Life and its furnishings were temporal and
on loan from the gods.
Kind of like those toys
you used to borrow from the library.
They all went back in the box,
ready for the next kid.

So, you could start by counting your losses.
Allowing them to find their place in the earth
and sky of your heart;
Filling the air with scent
And the ground with strength
for the journey ahead.
And it's normal to miss moments,

to miss people and seasons.
It's normal to cry
And let the salt water fall
to the edges of your mouth.

Some things, tough things, horrible things
May need holding again for a moment.
You know what I mean:
The pains you stuffed in your pockets
and have been walking with
for too long.
Once, they were too much to hold.
But something told you
You weren't ready to part ways.
When you are ready,
Reach down by your side,
Find these things,
and finish your conversation.
Say your peace.
Give them back.

No one who lives fully, lives light for long.
Every moment, day and season
Beckons us to hold on;
For life is dear, costly and thrilling.
And after you've counted your losses,
Let go.
Exhale.
Return borrowed goods.
Say your peace.
Maybe now
You can cross the threshold
into new beginnings.
Still you, but lighter for a moment.

Still you
But lighter
For a moment.

FROM YOUR KNEES

What is your unreachable summit?
The height you climb
And fall from
Clinging
And singing
Verses of overcoming
Yet falling
Nonetheless
Determined it should be
An easy ascent
As it is for so many
Others.

What is your unbeatable dragon?
The beast you fight
And bleed from
Fumbling
And stumbling for a sword
Yet losing
But still
Convinced it should be
An easy battle
As it is for so many
Others.

What is your unfathomable ocean?
The sea you sail
And retreat from
Weathered
And tethered
From endless horizon
Yet returning
Believing it should be
An easy journey
As it is for so many
Others.

These
Heights
Beasts
And Seas
Places of
Un-ease
That bring you
From your knees
Are not
Your enemies
(I repeat)
Are not
Your enemies

THE BRUTALITY OF BROKENESS

Beyond the brutality of brokenness
Beauty can be found
But only by those willing to look
Look through redeeming eyes.

Beyond the brutality of brokenness
A song can be heard
But only by those willing to listen
Listen through compassionate ears.

Some believe
God cannot stand
our brokenness and its copings.
But was the Christ not broken?
And has Trinity ever been anything
other
than
beautiful?

Therefore,
have you or I been anything
other
than
beautiful?

Beauty lies beyond the brutality of brokenness.

**

May we
have eyes
and ears
of love
with Trinity
to see this eternal truth.

FOUND ITS PLACE

One day
you may wake
to find
that pain
and its bearers
are gone.

But they are not.
Not really.

Grief;
It's still with you.
But now, the well it left in your deepest self
that you flooded with tears
and mourning
and stories
and filled to the brim,
found its life-giving place in the landscape
of your heart.

Sorrow;
It's still with you.
But now, the heavy lurking cloud overhead
that you stooped under
and weathered
and fought
and finally befriended,
found its rain-soaking place on the horizon
of your heart.

Humiliation;
It's still with you.
But now, the weighted earth and clay
that you fell into
and tasted
and wore
and took refuge in,
found its ground-breaking place in the valley
of your heart.

Shame;
It's still with you.
But now, the foreign garment of leaves
that you hid behind
and gathered
and fashioned
and replaced with skin,
found its shade-giving place in the garden
of your heart.

One day
you may wake
to find
that pain
and its bearers
are gone.

But they are not.
Not really.
They simply found their place.

THE LIGHT RESPONDED

When the Light came
All he kept in the shadows
Glittered and shone.
And shame rose.

"Why did I invite You?"
He asked the Light.
Doubting his decision.
Hating what he saw.

"You didn't invite me"
The Light responded.
"You followed me.
Followed me to liberty."

"Then why expose this stuff?"
He asked the Light.
Confused with this idea of freedom
That exposes shadow treasure.

"Freedom requires the work of truth."
The Light responded.
"And believing that I don't know
And we can't handle it
Never leads to life."

ON GOD

When I was about three years old, we lived on a busy street in a popular suburb of Melbourne, Australia. Our home was not far from a large supermarket and had a small iron gate low enough for me to hold the top of and peer over. With a big smile on his face, my father tells of how his young white-haired son David used to interrogate people walking past with their groceries. He tells of a time I had a lady unpack two entire bags of groceries and answer every question I had on what each item was. "She was there for quarter of an hour. And you were both loving every minute of it," he tells.

I like asking questions and discovering things. I find the world a fascinating place. I always have. You may imagine my initial fervour and excitement when I started my own personal journey of faith in 1995. I had so many questions about God and the afterlife, and my pastors had all the answers! Then, I discovered Christian bookstores. Even more answers! Then podcasts started appearing in my world. After that, YouTube.com. Before long, answers to questions were only a few clicks away. The little boy at the iron gate was having the time of his life!

But then, things stopped adding up. The promises the pastors made from the pulpit stopped working. Natalie and I suffered a confusing miscarriage. The traumatic birth of our beautiful daughter. Postnatal depression. Bankruptcy. A whole array of difficulties. And the God I'd come to know and believe in continued to fail me and miss my appointments. Like many, up until things stopped going my way, I had very little room for the mysteries of God. I only really had made space for the mastery. Religious mastery, to be precise.

I'm aware that if I write more here, it may be at risk of describing God in a way that is too concrete and sure. A concept which poetry most often avoids. For me, the journey to wholeness through the wilderness is more about finding beautiful questions that create life-giving moments where both myself and the Divine are loving every minute of discovering together.

THE WRESTLE

I found you
beyond
the 'why'
Far from
the 'why not'
Worlds from
the 'why me'

You held a space for me
beyond answers
to questions
my pain had
as if you knew
information was
never
going
to
heal
or resolve
or fix
my suffering.

Instead,
you agreed to wrestle
through many nights.
Never letting go.
Always with me
just like you promised.

Refusing to surrender,
I eventually realised
that wrestling with God
was not a crime.
That I was, in fact,
being held.
Being healed.
Being transformed by finding
you beyond answers.
Being blessed
by holding on to you
in my doubt and frustration
and never letting go.

And you never let go.
And you overcame me in the end.
And we both won.

KIND OF WAY

I know that you know.
So I should probably confess it.
Not because it's a bad thing,
but because it's normal
and necessary to admit
you've disappointed me
and continue to.
Although I don't mind as much
now.

Still, there were many times
I prayed.
Followed the rules.
Gave my two mites.
Did all the things I was told would work
and others certified
with charismatic conviction
to do more
give more
faith more
sacrifice more
lots more.

But still, nothing.
No breakthrough
like I believed,
like I prayed for.

I underestimated you.
I wanted to believe
you were containable
constrainable
and reliable
in the 'my way' kind of way.
The magician
hitman
slot machine
deal maker
earth shaker
genie-in-a-bottle
kind of way.

Then I recalled
that on a dark but necessary day
you took yourself
and my kind of way
and the cosmos
to a cross.
Then you went missing for three days,
And my world fell apart.

All my hope exhaled a forsaken surrender,
and my heart broke
and my dreams broke.
My kind of way
kind of died
again.

And there you were
alive and the same
but not really.
A resurrected form of you
that even took familiar friends
by surprise.

And that's what you keep doing.
To this day
you keep failing and disappointing me
in the best kind of ways.

Every time I think I've got you
where I think I need you
you disappoint and disappear
and turn up incognito
on a familiar path
at a regular meal
in an average garden
with a spark in your eye
that demands my attention.
You invite me again
to put my hand in your side,
embrace you and kiss you
and get to know you again
in a new kind of way.

THAT FIRE

That all-consuming fire you speak of,
does it hurt?
Is it as bad as some say,
or better?

Does it really burn away
all that doesn't belong?
All that's unlike you?
All that's not of your kind?
All that's not of love?

If I say yes to this fire,
could it take forever?
Could we go slow?
Could I change my mind?
Could it really help?

And when we're done,
am I still going to be me?
Am I going to feel complete?
Am I going to know we are one?
Am I going to be as alive as you say?

More importantly,
will you stay with me?
Will you hold my heart?
Will you lift your faces?
Will you cover me?

If this is your idea of fire,
refine me.

If this is the way you judge,
restore me.

If this is the lake you speak of,
baptise me.

If this is your invitation to oneness,
arrest me.

HEART AND MIND

'Open your heart'
'Open your mind'
But what does this mean?

For only by death
can they be closed.
And then... still.

Perhaps
heart and mind are not closed
but full.

Full of that which makes
little room
for hospitable guests
like compassion, mercy and grace.

Perhaps
heart and mind are not full
but dull.

Dull with a kind of
dark sadness
which comforted
unreconcilable pain long ago.

Perhaps
heart and mind are not dull
but hidden.

Hidden from maps
and those who wish
to cross their thresholds
with gifts of truth and belonging.

Heart and mind,
in your openness
may you be continually
emptied
brightened
and found.

Above all,
may you be given
the dignity and patience
you deserve, just as you are.

OH GOD

 "Oh God."
Five letters.
Two words.
One exhale.
Full stop.

"Oh God."
All my voice could say.
Trusting that my
very being
would fill in the detail.

"Oh God."
Hand over mouth.
Hand over heart.
Your hand over me
I hope.

"Oh God."
A prayer.
A cry.
A summons.
A summit.

"Oh God."
Five letters.
Two words.
One exhale.
Full stop.

THE DESCENT

All that kept me buoyant
became impossible to cling to.
It held me at the surface.
My head above water.
My lungs full.
My face bright.

But, I was sinking.

I assumed gravity would be merciful.
I thought that if I cried out
you would reach down
and pull me back to the surface.
Back to familiar surroundings.
Back to the life I had.

But my cries only summoned exhaustion.
My tears only added to the waters.
No lifeline from you.
No hand-up from the heavens.
The strength that bought me security
was failing.

I was sinking.

With heavy hope, I gave way to the descent.
The depths of despair were colder
and darker than I imagined.
My only possessions
were a pounding heart
and pressing questions.

How was I breathing underwater?
Why did the darkness feel familiar?
Where were you before?
And why did I get the sense
I was going to find treasure
no man could afford?

I had sunk.

The poor, the mourning
the meek, the hungry
all feast here with you.
This Eden on the ocean floor.
This terrifying
baptism of acceptance.

So, this is where you are?
In the company of lepers.
In this pit, this grave
this den of thieves.
Among those with little to offer
and those with nothing to lose.

I am home now.

I wish this great loss on no man.
Yet, I wish it for all.
For foundations are forged here.
And true selves discovered.
In currents of grief.
On the dark sand of suffering.

Still.

I still live on the surface.
Most days, anyway.
But its riches and offering
do not compare to the
brightly darkened treasure
held in the depths.
Found in the descent.

SO CLOSE

I have to say
it's been a challenge
developing a friendship
with those so close
they can be overlooked
and forgotten
on the best of days
and the worst.

Yet, there you are.
Three in one.
In all.
In me.

Clothed in creation.
Naked to heart's eyes.
Always conversing.
Attuned to heart's beat.

Christ in me.
The hope of glory.
Never leaving.
Always towards me.

Eternal life
I am assured and
breathing slowly knowing
I have forever to know You.

PARADOX OF DEFINITION

I have so much to say
so many words,
a lifetime of my own
a millennia of others.

Yet as I utter
and draw conclusions,
I draw a box
and put You in it.

And with religious zeal
I've defended that box,
forgetting I placed
eternity in there.

With past poets and prophets
I struggle to define You,
not wanting to confine You
but still compelled.

Compelled to express
the beauty and wonder
You are
and never cease to be.

Compelled to give witness
by weaving words
from twenty-six letters
strokes and spaces.

Perhaps like a lover's stare
silence says more
and frees You to speak
and define the edges.

The edges of the box
You are beyond,
the edges of the cosmos
as it expands in You.

The edges of my inner world
with its rocky refusal
to accept the shameful parts
Grace has defined as acceptable.

Oh YHVH
how patient You are
with Your own children
as we learn
to be loved
beyond comprehension,
imagination or interpretation
of You.

AND YOU WAIT

I wanted to do my own thing.
And You let me.
After all,
You gave me this will.
This floundering will
that gives me
a sense of me
a sense of control
a sense of choice.

And You wait.

You wait like a father who gives
his girl a new bike
and she goes missing
for hours.

You wait like a father who gives
his son his inheritance
knowing he'll make a mess
of things.

And You wait.

You wait on the street till dusk,
sure that she'll come home
before the darkness sets in.

You wait at the gate and run
when you see his sunken soul
stagger into the city.

And You welcome.

You welcome the strong-of-will.
The rebellious heart.
The limit-tester.
The boundary-pusher.
The bankrupt and broken.
You welcome any will
that comes home,
even for a short time.

You welcome me.

Your door is always open,
as are your arms.
The feast forever prepared.
Tears of joy ready to cross the threshold
of Your cheeks.

Father, Son and Spirit.
Creator of wills.
Your imitable will to love
and forgive
compels creation
to do the same.

TRINITY IS

Trinity is union.
A constant conversation.
A becoming belonging.
A covenantal choice.
A joyful expression.

Trinity is union.
A perichoresis of three.
A oneness of flow.
A convergence of rivers.
A swimmable source.

Trinity is union.
A bonded togetherness.
An eternal alarming reminder.
An invitation
to echo its way
on earth
as it is in heaven.

DISPLACE DARKNESS

Displace darkness.

As he whispered
it resonated,
not as a gentle breeze
but as a hurricane
through my already
turbulent soul.

"What else
have you called me to do?"
I asked,
expecting further instruction.

-silence-

That's it?
Yes
But, how?
Come, follow me

CONTROL

How on earth
Are you in control
of everything
on earth?

Do you control seas?
And winds?
And poets?
And plagues?

Do you control kings?
And wars?
And fires?
And fortune?

Do you control love?
And hate?
And strength?
And sickness?

I think not.

Powerful you are,
No doubt.
And omnipotent enough
To refrain from usurping
A world you made powerful
And wills you made free.

AS A CHILD

How is it
Hope comes like this?
As a child
Fragile and vulnerable

How is it
Love comes like this?
As a child
Unrelenting and unrestrained

How is it
Salvation comes like this?
As a child
Innocent and inclusive

How is it
God comes like this?
As a child

And how do I
Respond to this magnificent absurdity?
As a child

THIS TEMPLE

This messy temple
is not much to look at
no handmade stained glass
but child-made stained clothes.

This skin covered temple
is no high cathedral
no ancient wonder
but still filled with awe.

This divine temple
is no sacred place
no breathtaking beauty
but still taking breath.

This living temple
is no church to thousands
no place of worship
but worship made flesh.

Forever, the Divine
has made our hearts their home
and Three-in-One will dwell
in us all
all in us.

ON EMPATHY

Several years ago, I took a personal profiling test which confirmed something I was suspicious of. That is, I'm highly empathetic. In fact, the outcome revealed I was in the top percentile among others across the globe who had participated in the same test.

Not long before this, I had come across Dr. Elaine Aron's work around Highly Sensitive People; a nervous system trait that effects twenty percent of the world's population. I took her test and rated high as an HSP (Highly Sensitive Person). I was both relieved and disappointed. Relieved that I wasn't a weirdo who had a strange ability to sit with others in their pain and cry their tears because they didn't know how to. Disappointed that I was in my late thirties and only now realising why much of life's heaviness I felt was not my own. Actually, I wasn't just disappointed, I was downright pissed-off. As an Aussie lad, when very high empathy is part of your design and these giftings and traits are not acknowledged and managed, it can be a challenge to make your way through life without healthy ways to manage the overwhelm.

Since discovering these treasures, I've been able to make necessary changes to promote better health and boundaries. Poetry has come as a gift to help me metabolise and process experiences quicker than before, along with some beautiful contemplative prayer practices.

The following poems begin with several I've written from a posture of empathy.

The three pieces on Who Took Your Voice came to me several hours after waking up to a text from my new friend Wm. Paul Young who text me from the US saying, "Title for a poem or song: Who Took Your Voice." The two Poems for Glenn were written for a mentor and friend, who in late 2019, lost his nineteen-year-old son to complications which arose from an unforeseen brain aneurism. I'm grateful for the opportunity to include them here.

In confession, I feel some of these pieces are not mine. Instead, my soul heard unspoken cries from others, and I had the privilege of weaving words around them.

THE BURDEN BEARER – Piece 1

Most of it came uninvited.
It crept in
and swept in
like dust and dirt
over the threshold
of invitation.

Somewhere between
your conception
and now
the heaviness
took up residence
without warning;
weaving itself
into the fabric of
your being.

It wasn't meant to be this way.
This weary way.
This somewhere between
lost-and-found way.
This keep-it-all-to-yourself way.
And even though you bore it all,
so much
is simply not
your fault.
Not at all.

Heaven knows
you were only
trying to make
things work.
Trying to keep
the peace
by holding the chaos
close to your chest.

If anything,
you should know
that the same strength
it takes
to carry
burdens and shame
not belonging to you
is the same strength needed
to let go
and let God.
You have that strength.

If anything,
you should know
that you'll walk lighter
and wiser than most;
albeit with a limp
and a lamp
to light the way
for others weighed down
to be free.
To be free.

THE BURDEN BEARER – *Piece 2*

Somewhere
early in life
you discovered
that you had
the capacity
and compassion
to carry
burdens
and blows.

So, all
that came
towards you
from the world
and those in it
that had
nowhere to land,
you absorbed
and made room for.

You held
it all
in yourself.
All the pain
and promises.
All the chaos
and care.
All the shame
and secrets.

So, body
and bones
and breath
held the
stories
and the score
for favour
and fear.

Then somewhere
about now
you're done.
Finished storing
burden bearing
and over-caring.
Sick and tired
of saving
and sin-eating.

Let go
and make room,
weary one.
The world
is too big
to carry.
Take stock
vacate spaces
that store troubles.

All yours
and theirs
Let
(Inhale)
It
(Exhale)
All
(Inhale)
Go
(Exhale)

INVISIBLE INJURY

I didn't judge you
when you fell sick
with the virus
after the long flight home.

I didn't shame you
when you couldn't walk
without crutches
after the severe car accident.

I didn't avoid you
when you couldn't breathe
without an oxygen mask
after the minor stroke.

I didn't pressure you
when you couldn't talk
without a slur
after the jaw reconstruction.

So, please don't judge me
when I leave the party
without warning.
It's the anxiety.

Please don't shame me
when you need to talk
but I just can't.
It's the burnout.

Please don't avoid me
when I can't walk
without cloudy countenance.
It's the depression.

Please don't pressure me
when I can't tell you why
I feel fragile like I do.
It's the PTSD.

**

It takes a compassionate heart
and patient witness
to honour another's invisible injury.
For like outer injuries of the body
few choose them
but many steward them.
God, help us all to love
and judge not.

MY STORY

This is my story
with its sharp edges
dark corners
secret passageways
and remnant bones in closets.

This is my story
with its high lofts
and dark basements
I fell and flew into
so many times.

This is my story
built by bodies
measured by masses
coloured by crowds
renovated by bearers of good news.

What is your story?

Tell me
of the tales
that shaped
the abode
of your soul.

Tell me
of the times
tragedy overstayed
and triumph
left without warning.

Tell me
of the days
courage cooked you breakfast
and grief
kept the kettle on.

Tell me
how you managed
to stop the dark nights
from giving you stars
to navigate by.

Tell me
where you found
the strength to forgive
those who were as
undeserving as you.

Tell me your story
for I want to know
how your soul-story and mine
are mysteriously bound
by the Author of Life.

Tell me your story.
Tell me my story.
Tell me our story.

TENDER HEART

When you foster your tender heart
Rich experience appears on life's palette
And you paint with vivid expression

In one minute
You may find yourself
Beholding beauty and horror

In one hour
You may find yourself
Weeping tears of joy and sorrow

In one day
You may find yourself
Swinging between paralysis and elation

In one month
You may find yourself
Celebrating both life and death

In one lifetime
You
May
Find
Your
Self
   When you foster your tender heart

WHO TOOK YOUR VOICE – Piece 1

Maybe
your 'no'
was not enough
and Dominance
pushed it aside
like it was never there.
And you learnt
your words
didn't matter.

Maybe
your silence
was required
and Coercion
whispered its lie
that secrets were safer.
And you learnt
that truth
equalled pain.

Maybe
your story
was cut short
and Shame
covered your mouth
to filter in the darkness.
And you learnt
to only
be positive.

Maybe, now that you are safe,
the older, stronger you
can stand beside
the little one inside
and begin to ask,
'Who took your voice?'

Maybe, you were not created
to have your boundaries crossed
and your no dishonoured.

Maybe, you were not created
to hold all those secrets
and all that pain.

Maybe, you were not created
to tell a partial story
in order to be
entirely accepted.

WHO TOOK YOUR VOICE – Piece 2

Who took your voice
with all its tone
and volume
and beauty
of pain
and joy
and expression of you?

Who took your voice
with all its colour
and silence
and pauses
of rhythm
and pace
and music of you?

Who took your voice
when you exhaled
to show
and tell
of trauma
and secret
and treatment of you?

Did it remain inside?
Was it muffled outside?
Dismissed?
Minimised?
Was it met with contempt
by those with too much to lose
and little to give?

Come now,
one
word
at
a
time.
Like the healed leper
it's time
to take up your voice
and talk.

WHO TOOK YOUR VOICE – Piece 3

You didn't mean to lose it
but when you went to use it
it wasn't there,
and you began to wonder
who took your voice.

There was a story to tell
when you experienced hell
but lips didn't open,
and you began to wonder
who took your voice.

You don't remember giving it away.
It's like it was stolen

but not stolen
because you can speak

but not about that event
or pain
or doubt
or skeletons in your closet.

Maybe that's it?!
You have a voice
but you can't find an ear
to hear
with love
the truth
of what is
and was
and shame
and hurt
and...so

...so, may it be
that your voice
finds the attuned ear of
a co-suffering other
who'll sing in harmony
the songs of deliverance
you need to sing.

A POEM FOR GLENN

Rest now
Find your place
In the midst of things
In loving memory
In the hearts of many

Rest now
Find your peace
Amongst the loved
Alongside the fallen
Amidst the resurrected

Rest now
Find release
From days unlived
From goals unmet
From arms which held you

Rest now
Find your rhythm
With choirs of angels
With Trinity's dance
With all creation

Rest now
      Rest

ANOTHER POEM FOR GLENN
- YOUR HAND IN MINE

I have a photo in my phone
Of your hand in mine
I still can't share it without tears

Even when the nurse splinted it for the drip
We insisted on holding on

Sitting for days by your side
Vigilantly waiting for a sign
Or answered prayer for relief
Something
Anything

As we walked from the ward for the last time
I never realised till later
I'd never touch you again

Now, I'd ransom the world
Just to hear you breathe
To embrace you
Or simply sight you across the room

And I know we'll see you later
But your eternity is subject to my clock
And it seems like so long till then

In the meantime,
I'll hold your mother's love-engraved hand
Your sister's and brother's too
In tight hope
And loving memory
Of your hand in mine

THE CONVOCATION

You flew as far as the tether allowed.
Its pull on your leg
a reminder
you needed to return
to the safety of not seeing.

For years the way things were
were the way they were
until the familiar terrain
and the cage you called home
felt too small for your restless heart.

You knew the cord around your ankle
had worn so thin
that if the wild's call was strong
and the wind was in your favour
you could break free.

And you did,
Free Spirit.

Far lands knew your name.
The warm sun invited you in.
New air stretched out your lungs.
So you flew home
to tell your soul's mate.

Perhaps you'd expected too much
from those that felt they'd lost you.
Maybe your free return was not enough
to show your love
for both home and horizon.

Fear and trembling filled the place
that the cord left behind.
Making it hard to feel free
when you went looking for your self
in the wilderness.

And you did,
Free Spirit.

Again, these ties lost their strength
as yours increased
and every new part of you,
although not welcomed by some,
found a convocation in your heart.

Look down, Free Spirit.
Note how high and far you've flown.
See now, at your ankle
the many frayed cords.
Note how loved and whole you are.

note how loved and whole you are

David Tensen

ON BOUNDARIES

It's not uncommon that highly sensitive and empathetic persons find themselves caught up in the well-disguised complex webs of co-dependency and rescuing. It's rarely intentional. It's often just something we can wrap our ego and identity around early enough in life. After all, we think, *who doesn't want to be the person others boast about for being there and bringing great healing?*

I don't think helping others is a bad thing at all, it's just not very sustainable long-term unless the desire and tendencies are acknowledged, welcomed, addressed and stewarded well.

At their worst, addicted rescuers, like me, walk as unhealthy wounded healers until they see how costly their ways are to themselves and others. Then, one day, if they are fortunate enough, they discover the gift of boundaries and begin the process of breaking their addiction. Following the previous poems on empathy, these few pieces were written from a place of recognition and recovery, which I'm still on.

THE RESCUER

When I'm present to you,
to your story,
to your trials and triumphs –
I'm not with me. I'm with you.

When we are navigating the
tear-fed seas of your traumatic tales,
I'm not at home –
I'm out. Out with you.

When, together, we trek through
recall and reason,
only to find ourselves lost again –
it's a dark march back to me.

Many times now, I have strayed far from me.
Far from familiar.
And I've hitch-hiked through healing.
I've stumbled through dark heartlands
looking for myself.
Attempting to untangle my story from yours.
Finding and binding the armour I gave away
when your vulnerability
took you too close to the edge of yourself.

So, please, pardon me.
Forgive me when I pull back,
fall down,
collapse,
go missing,
and need help.
For I am a recovering rescuer.

And as one who limps with aid
after having hip touched by an angel,
I am learning now
how to move with strong boundaries
and fierce refusals.

I am learning to walk without
leaving myself behind.

WATER STORIES

Its unending waters stream from life-temples.
Mine. Yours.
Our stories held together by banks,
they form a river.
A river we fill with words and deeds,
Waters we leave behind.

For some
the sacred waters of another's story
are treacherous
rivers to wade into.

A cry for help beckons us
into its flow,
into its ancient current.
Rescue efforts from the edge
reap slim rewards.

Tethered words
of encouragement and reason
to the drowning heart-parts
fail like a lifeline too short.

We must go in.

Must I go in?
Again, I stand at the bank.
At the threshold of discomfort.

Knowing that I can't un-know.
Knowing that it may take hours
or days to dry off.

I can't help it.
I'm already knee deep.
I absorb. I engage.
I laugh and mourn.
I'm already in over my head.

I am embarrassed to say
that I've lost myself in many waters,
needing rescuing myself.

Empathy has become both
strength and weakness,
an Achilles heel.

Lord, teach me to swim
for I live at the water's edge,
and the edge lives in me.

SPINNING ON EMPTY

Please show me
How on earth
I can empty myself for others
Without losing myself in others
The way you three do so well

I'm still not good at it

You see, I overdo it
Then, I underdo it

I check in
and leave too much of myself in the room.
I check out
not even gracing the door to begin with.

God,
how do you do it?

How do you empty your selves
and stay full
all at the same time?

Like circular breathing

Like an ever-spinning wheel

Like a trusted lover's embrace

Like a circular dance of three

Pushing and pulling
Pushing and pulling
Pushing and pulling

Always spinning on empty

LETTERS

I don't remember how or why, but I discovered that if I wrote to my emotions and experiences in a personified way, the words would come easier and hold more meaning. Some of these pieces carry threads of previous poems in their language and rhythm. Others are shorter and at one time, I considered excluding from the publication. But perhaps they are just what someone needs to read.

ELDERS

The campfire-till-coal talks
The long-ride-home talks
The coffees-until-closing talks
These are the conversations my generation thirsts
for.

Elders, where are you?

Why are you not listening?
When did you get stuck?
Where does it hurt?
Who told you that your scars
and tears and unveiled fears were worthless?
For they are priceless.

Elders, where are you?

Please, don't reach down for relevance.
Don't slow down or stop on life's journey
through valleys of darkness and death.
We need to know what happens next.

Elders, where are you?

Has materialism won your heart?
Has accumulation bewitched you?
Has security stolen your courage?
Please, tell us we're wrong.

Elders, where are you?

Or, are we not looking, or asking, or listening
for your wise ways?
Have we been blinded by youthful hubris and
rugged independence?
Have our silent cries been silenced by roaring
progress into loftiness?

Elders, where are you?

Please, make yourselves known.
Seek us. Find us.
And we can grow up together.
Old together.
Wise together.
Elders together.

DEAR STRENGTH

Why have you not returned to me,
my Strength?
I need you back for good, my Strength.
But you only visit on occasion.
Why?

What are you doing,
my Strength?
I had plans for us, my Strength.
But you stood me up, again.
Why?

We used to do so much together,
my Strength.
We made so much work, my Strength.
We were esteemed by so many.
Remember?

I've been with Weakness
for ages now, it seems.
Sure, she's gentle and present
but that's what's so frustrating.

Recently, Wisdom told me that
it's Weakness's turn.
That you won't return until Weakness can stay.
Is that true, my Strength?

Wisdom says I should accept Weakness
and all her qualities.
That Weakness is needed for wholeness
and I can't keep ignoring her beauty.

My Strength, I need a favour.
In your stead can you send someone else?
Could you let Courage know that
I need her for one thing?

Wisdom tells me I need Courage
to make Weakness *my* Weakness.
Because those who embrace their Weakness
are indeed the most courageous.

Please, my Strength, hurry.
And get Patience ready too;
I feel that she'll be needed next.

DEAR BREAKDOWN

Dear Breakdown,

When I saw you coming
over the horizon
I braced myself.

With your strong gaze
and constant gait
I began to suspect
you were on assignment
or I had summoned you
unknowingly.

I'd seen what you
had done to others.
Their lives resembled wrecks.
Many lost hope and
all sense of pride.
You were coming
for me now,
and I was unprepared.

Sure, those people recovered
and discovered
they couldn't arrange galaxies
with their false personas.
But who wants to go through hell for
that lesson?

And yes, some claimed
they loved deeper
laughed louder
and found their true selves.
But who wants to submit to your
painful ways?

So much in me
told me
you were not welcome.
Too many memories
of failing and falling
had me questioning your nearness
once more.

But then
you had your way.

I expected you to hit and run
but you were more
committed than that.
I had you all wrong.
Sure, it hurt.
And sure, I died many deaths.
But you allowed me to see
that I was never in charge,
never that strong,
never going to wake up
to the Presence of all things
unless you came
to my rescue.
So, thank you,
Breakdown.
Thank you.

thank you

DEAR INSTRUCTION

Dear Instruction,

How do you feel about being used and
consumed as such?
Like gloves on a surgeon, you are so often
discarded once used.
Like product packaging, so often you are an
afterthought.
An obstacle to overcome in order to reach the
end.

But without you, we'd be lost. Right?
Like driving through a foreign land without
GPS.
Like classrooms minus teachers and books.
We really have undervalued your place in our
lives.

Instruction, it seems that you've had some
fierce competition: Pride.
Pride beats you to assemble Ikea cupboards but
only leads to embarrassing 'nailed it' memes.
Pride outshines you in marriage
but rarely does it promote meaningful
connection.

Instruction, you are the long and winding road
to the summit.
And if there was a shortcut, you'd know.

Instruction, we are sorry.
Can we be friends again?

DEAR TEARS

There you are
Just under my breath.
A part of me so fragile
it's dressed in a salty sea
of surf that breaks against
the back of my eyes, like generous
waves knocking against a vessel's bow.

This crafted vessel
is the self I sail in most days.
It's the me that moves at pace
and cuts through seas
of tears and tenderness.

Until the wind dies.

And there you are.
A swell birthed from miles away.
Days. Weeks. Years ago, even.
Waves that have been waiting for me.
Waiting for a moment
of exhaustion
of truth
of surrender
of stillness.

It's strange how your waters
bring such momentum.
More so than the wind I work for.

Still, I don't know why I refuse your help.
You seem to know where I should be going
much better than I.

You seem to be on my side
guiding me to lost treasures
of resolve, rest and relief.

Tears, thank you.
You are the better navigator.
You are the kinder force.

May I be mindful of your knock.
The ebb and flow of my breathing.
And make way for your coming
more often.

DEAR JOY

I'm not sure why
you think it's appropriate
to turn up in such a dark hour
but I'm glad you're here.

There's not a lot
to be happy about
as I can't bear the thought
of this being my tomorrow.

But still, you waltz in
with that cheeky smile on your face
that says everything
your lips needn't say.

I'm still puzzled on
how your very presence
gives me strength
but somehow, it does.

I must say, joy,
I do love how incarnational you are.
How you've been here before.
How you're okay with my pain.
How you give my suffering the space it needs.
And how you cut through
a jungle of fear
and hold my angst,
like it belongs.

Reminding me again
that I do too.

DEAR CHURCH

Dear Church,

I've struggled to visit your gatherings.
Not because you hurt me,
but because you held so much hurt.

And I had the hardest time ignoring it.
Even though you wouldn't see it,
the hurt kept leaking into my lap.

And it became impossible to undo.
Your pain and mine combined,
were too much for me to fix.

And that's what I've had to dismantle
the lie that we can be separated.
The lie that it's my job.

To fix and save all I see and sense.
The lie that you're unaffected
when I hurt too.

So now I'm unsure of how we can dance again.
But you'll find me in the shadows,
slowly moving towards the centre again.

slowly
moving

ON LIFE

After the relationship with ourselves and God is altered, it's not uncommon that we see the world differently. Not better, just different.

These final few pieces were penned over the past two years. There are several on parenting. Others on time. And a couple on forgiveness and vows.

Soap Film Prayer was written during the 2020 COVID-19 crisis.

HELD

"Dad, I'm gay."
Confessed the young man
And his father embraced him
Just as he'd always done

"Mum, I'm gonna be a single mum."
Confessed the young woman
And her mother embraced her
Just as she'd always done

"Dad, I don't agree with the notion of a literal
hell."
Confessed the young man
And his father embraced him
Just as he'd always done

"Mum, I don't know if I believe in God anymore."
Confessed the young woman
And her mother embraced her
Just as she'd always done

"Dad, I've enrolled to study climate science."
Confessed the young woman
And her father embraced her
Just as he'd always done

"Dad, I'm moving overseas to start a family."
Confessed the young man
And his father embraced him
Just
as
he'd
always
done

THAT PHOTO OF YOU ON YOUR FIRST DAY AT SCHOOL

When I look at that photo of you
on your first day at school;
I mean, really look at it;
I see myself.

I see
A young
Wide-eyed
Slightly-scared
Smiling-for-the-photo
Knot-in-my-stomach
No-idea-on-what's-coming
Part of me
That has never really disappeared.

Sure, I may be projecting.
It may even be misplaced empathy.

But THAT look!

I've seen it in the mirror.
I've felt it
Moved with it
Fought it
And I still do.
Still, today

Those same eyes look back at me
Before presentations
Before plane flights
Before tough conversations
In fact...
I saw those eyes in my own reflection
When I left your classroom
And peered back through the window
To see if you were OK.
If WE were OK.

Like you, I tried my darnedest
To be brave
Be strong
Not cry too much
And keep going.

I tried, anyway.
Because
I hate to be a bother
To those who love me
Because
What can they do?
There is no simple fix.
No pep-talk platitude.
No magic kiss.
No satisfying distraction.
Not much other than
Hugs
Time
And permission
To be myself.

So perhaps,
Perhaps,
As your parent
I could just
Let you
Be your own self.

Perhaps
I could just
Give you the gift
Of my adult presence
To let you know
That 'you got this'
And 'it's gonna be OK'.

And at the same time
Perhaps I could learn
To allow the child in me
To hold your hand
On the way to class
To let you know
That I REALLY DO know
What it's like
To be where you are.

And maybe,
Just maybe,
After many walks to class
And uniformed farewells;
The child in me
Will find their peace.
And the adult in you
Will emerge.

A GOOD ONTOLOGY

I do not have to BE good
I do not need hell to BE good
I simply am
by virtue of
my existence
good

I AM good
because I BElong
and
I am BEloved
BEyond BElief
BEyond BEhaviour
by three that agree
that I AM
in them
altogether
good

(Opening line in memory of poet Mary Oliver 1935-2019)

UNTIL YOU FORGIVE

You can't cross over
until you've been crossed
and have to forgive
to stay grounded.

You can't move on
until you've been floored
and have to forgive
to keep going.

You can't make it work
until you've screwed it all up
and have to forgive
to fix it.

You can't soldier on
until you've been in wars
and have to forgive
to find peace.

You can't be yourself
until you've faced your own shadow
and have to forgive
to be whole.

David Tensen

I WANT TO BE

I want to be a kind friend to myself.
A forgiving and generous friend.

I want to be a good boss to myself.
A gracious and considerate boss.

I want to be a gentle teacher to myself.
A passionate and curious teacher.

I want to be a loving parent to myself.
A patient and encouraging parent.

I want to be a spacious world to myself.
A compassionate and abundant world.

TIME

Waiting is not wasting time
But you may feel time is wasted
Because you hold time
Like it's a commodity
You are a steward of

But time waits for no man
So it need not be master
Or slave

In fact
Time offers a hand of friendship
And promises to be
An ever-present companion
Always marking steps
Always building expectation
Always making the promise clearer
Always walking with you towards the future
Faithfully drawing the end closer
To you both

THE SEEN PARENT

Heaven sees you
as you lay
all scrunched up
on that toddler's bed
because it's the only way
you can hold
your sick child
through darkness
until dawn.

Heaven sees you
as you check again
for nits
by lamplight
all the while scratching
your own head
praying it's all in your
head.
But not.

Heaven sees you
regret when you can't
make that parade
because life happens
siblings happen
but you long
to lock eyes
and smile
with pride.

Heaven sees you
wash, hang, fold
repeat
buy, cook, clean
repeat
day after day after day
because parents do that
for children
they love.

Heaven sees you
make the most with
what you have
and have not.
With what was given
and never had.
For heaven knows
your story
and sees you.

COMPANI

come
break bread with me
let us imagine
neither you nor I
own anything
but together
are responsible
for everything

STILL

Wind in sails gone
Out at sea now
Moved by tides and swell
Still, very much alive

Tired of paddling
Lungs hurt from blowing
Land in sight
Desperately need relief

Poems blow in
When the wind dies
When I can hear my heart beat
When the ink runs low

NEVER VOWED

Like fingers on hot iron
Hand withdrawn
Wrist held
Burn assessed
Lesson learned
Vow made
Never again
Yet, not every iron is on
But still
Be careful

Like dinner date declined
Heart withdrawn
Chest held
Shame assessed
Lesson learned
Vow made
Never again
Yet, not every request is rejected
But still
Be careful

Like absent father's constant excuses
Hope withdrawn
Tears held
Worth assessed
Lesson learned
Vow made
Never again
Yet, not every dad disregards his own
But still
Be careful

PERFECT DAD

You didn't have a perfect dad
because such a man does not exist.
Because such a child does not exist.

And every dad was once the child
of an imperfect man
who was also once a child.

No, there is no excuse for abuse.
But there is room for growth
and it never all happens in one man.
It's generational.
Incremental.
Situational.
Environmental.
Accidental
and intentional.

Dads, if you are holding on to shame
and regret, what-ifs, and oh shits,
let it go.
Forgive yourself. Be gracious to you.
Your sins have most likely punished you enough.
No need to beat yourself up more.

And children, adult children reading this.
Let's be adults and let it go.

Acknowledge the effort. Seek the gold.
Accept the failings of your imperfect parent
and forgive him.

For in doing so, you can accept your failings,
and find freedom to fail again
into a better future.

THE PAST

When we turn a new page,
determined to start a new chapter,
the witness of 'what was'
waves goodbye
and folds in on history.

And there, What Was remains.
Pressed.
Bound.
Part of a sacred fellowship
called The Past.

Many have failed to see
that The Past is a strong force.
Shaping tomorrow
from the shadows
with a majority vote.

Sometimes
we bookmark The Past.
Referencing selective stories
for a sameness
and sympathy.

But singular pages wear thin.
The strongest stories
are the sealed ones.
Bleeding
and unreconciled.
Silently and violently
mattering.

The truth is,
dismembered accounts
can only be made whole
when we choose
to courageously
re-member
The Past
without partiality.

SOAP FILM PRAYER

My prayer is that
when the soap film is washed
from every hand
we appear from our dwellings
with cleaner hearts
wider arms
and eyes so bright
we see the beauty
in every good thing.

My prayer is that
when the soap film is washed
from every hand
we find ourselves grounded
with tender hearts
loving arms
and eyes so healed
we see our worth
in a stranger's smile.

My prayer is that
when the soap film is washed
from every hand
we emerge compassionate people
with forgiving hearts
generous arms
and eyes so open
we see no problem
in fickle inconvenience.

My prayer is that
when the soap film is washed
from every hand
we fall into the gift of us
with fragile hearts
binding arms
and eyes so kind
we see through darkness
into all we could be.

As a kind of bookend, I'd like to finish with the same blessing I opened with. Thank you for journeying with me.

A BLESSING FOR THE HEART JOURNEY

Today, fellow fallers,
recoverers, rescuers,
winners, losers,
famous and infamous,
I bless you.

The runners and the lame,
the bankrupt and billionaires,
the saints and sinners,
the lost and lonely,
I bless you.

I bless you with knowing
that the journey of a thousand steps
will be paved by
potholes,
sinkholes,
assholes,
and whatever
it takes to make
you whole.
Because you are human.

I bless you with knowing
that the invitation
to face the world
with an unveiled face
may be done at your pace,
or never at all.
Because it's an invitation.

But know this:
By love and choice
Trinity's unmasked face
shines upon you
and is gracious to you.
Trinity lifts up their faces towards you
and offers you peace.
Because you belong.

THE WRESTLE
Also available in eBook and Audiobook format.

w: www.davidtensen.com
e: david@davidtensen.com

ig: @david_tensen
fb: /davidtensenwriter
tw: @davidtensen

CPSIA information can be obtained
at www.ICGtesting.com
Printed in the USA
LVHW041357151120
671606LV00007B/276

9 780648 989325